TO Nic

Confirmation.

Love,

Charlie

Listening to God

with Padre Pio

Listening to God

with Padre Pio

Compiled by
EILEEN DUNN BERTANZETTI

Our Sunday Visitor Publishing Division
Our Sunday Visitor, Inc.
Huntington, Indiana 46750

Nihil Obstat
Msgr. Michael Heintz, Ph.D.
Censor Librorum

Imprimatur
✠ Kevin C. Rhoades
Bishop of Fort Wayne-South Bend
February 23, 2011

The *Nihil Obstat* and *Imprimatur* are official declarations that a book is free from doctrinal or moral error. It is not implied that those who have granted the *Nihil Obstat* and *Imprimatur* agree with the contents, opinions, or statements expressed.

The Scripture passages that follow Padre Pio's quotations are taken from the *Catholic Edition of the New Revised Standard Version of the Bible* (NRSV), copyright © 1989 and 1993 by the Division of Christian Education of the National Council of the Churches of Christ in the United States of America. Used by permission. All rights reserved.

Every reasonable effort has been made to determine copyright holders of excerpted materials and to secure permissions as needed. If any copyrighted materials have been inadvertently used in this work without proper credit being given in one form or another, please notify Our Sunday Visitor in writing so that future printings of this work may be corrected accordingly.

ISBN: 978-1-59276-132-6 (Inventory No. T1188)
LCCN: 2011922452

Cover design: Rebecca J. Heaston
Cover art: Wittman
Interior design: Dianne Nelson

PRINTED IN THE UNITED STATES OF AMERICA

CONTENTS

INTRODUCTION

PADRE PIO — FATHER PIO — bore the stigmata, the five ever-bleeding wounds of Christ Crucified, in his hands, feet, and side for fifty years. Through his many gifts, including healing, reading of souls, and counseling, he was used by God to bring help and comfort and healing to the millions who sought him during his long life. He often assured people that he would do even more for them after he died than while on earth, because then he would be so much nearer to the Source of Life, Jesus Christ. So if you need a counselor, rescuer, prayer warrior, healer, or friend, call on St. Padre Pio.

Padre Pio always told people, "Send me your guardian angel with any prayer requests you have, and I'll do what I can for you." No matter how young or old you are, my friend, you have a guardian angel, so you, too, can send your angel to Padre Pio with your requests. While awaiting your answers from heaven, remember that St. Pio often said, "Pray, hope, and don't worry," because Jesus Christ is always with you, and so what do you need to fear?

If many of Padre Pio's messages seem to focus on suffering, it is because in his great love for everyone, he felt everyone's pain, whether moral, physical, or mental. He wanted to share their pain and help to alleviate it through his intercessory prayers, through his gifts of healing and reading of souls, and through his own endless suffering due to the ever-bleeding stigmata.

Now canonized, since 2002, Padre Pio is among the "holy company" he often spoke about — that holy company of saints, both on earth and in heaven. As he advised, "Let us never take our eyes off them or we shall never be able to reach them; we shall be deprived of those secret treasures which they alone possess and shall be excluded from the eternal joy." It is my prayer that you will find, in this little book you hold, many of "those secret treasures," and that they will lead you along your life's journey and help you to live always in peace and joy, in God's merciful Heart.

Why not take a moment now and ask Padre Pio to be your spiritual guide as you prayerfully read this little book? As he said, "Speak to me always, when Jesus wants, and with confidence and sincerity, being certain of finding in me someone who understands well his children's weakness, and who is full of goodwill to help them."

While you are speaking to him, ask Padre Pio to accept you as his spiritual child — no matter your age — and to lead, guide, comfort, and love you as you prayerfully read this little book. After all, if on earth he had the gift of bilocation — the ability to be in more than one place at one time — surely he can be near you right now, if you simply call on him. You will find, even if you read only a few lines of this book each day, that God's loving presence will slowly but surely — through Padre Pio's intercession — change your life and give you joy, peace, and inner security. You will be more accepting of your sufferings, knowing that Jesus suffers right along with you — and for you.

Let Mary, the mother of Christ, be your "star," as St. Pio says, and let Padre Pio be your priest, your friend, and your guide. He is mine, and I have no regrets, not when the path always leads me to Jesus, my Lord and my God.

— Eileen Dunn Bertanzetti

Notes to the Reader

I have made every effort to use St. Padre Pio's lesser-known quotations, especially quotations that I haven't used in my previous books about him, published by Our Sunday Visitor, Pauline Books & Media, and The Word Among Us Press. Except for a few minor changes in order to maintain the clarity of Padre Pio's words for the reader, everything herein, from his *Letters*, is verbatim.

A Special Acknowledgment

I would like to thank acquisitions editor Jackie Lindsey for all the support she has given me through all these years working together. She has been a beautiful role model, mentor, and friend.

1. JESUS

JESUS KEEPS NOTHING FOR Himself of what is done for love of Him, and He will repay us very lavishly. Don't let us make our happiness depend on enjoying wonderful health, or else we should be just like those foolish worldly people to whom it is not given to know the secrets of heaven.... Continue to love Jesus, and make an effort to love Him more and more, without wanting to know anything else. He alone will steer us to the haven of salvation.

"This Jesus is
  'the stone that was rejected by you, the builders;
    it has become the cornerstone.'
There is salvation in no one else, for there is no other name under heaven given among mortals by which we must be saved."

— ACTS 4:11-12

2. SHE WHO HUMBLED HERSELF

I IMPLORE YOU TO BE faithful and humble and always to keep the great Mother of God before your mental gaze, she who humbled herself more profoundly the more she was exalted.

Never, ever be exalted at your virtues, but repeat that everything comes from God, and give Him the honor and glory.

Or do you suppose that it is for nothing that the scripture says, "God yearns jealously for the spirit that he has made to dwell in us"? But he gives all the more grace; therefore it says,

"God opposes the proud,
    but gives grace to the humble."
Submit yourselves therefore to God. — JAMES 4:5-7

3. HIS VOICE

I AM GREATLY COMFORTED AND very content in Jesus' company, and who could describe the help it is to me to have Him continually by my side? This company makes me much more careful not to do anything which would displease God. It seems to me as if Jesus is constantly watching me. If it sometimes happens that I lose the presence of God, I soon hear Our Lord calling me back my duty. I cannot describe the voice He uses to call me back, but I know that it is very penetrating, and the soul who hears it finds it almost impossible to refuse what He asks.

"The gatekeeper opens the gate for him, and the sheep hear his voice. He calls his own sheep by name and leads them out. When he has brought

out all his own, he goes ahead of them, and the sheep follow him because they know his voice. They will not follow a stranger, but they will
run from him because they do not know the voice of strangers.... Very
truly, I tell you, I am the gate for the sheep. All who came before me are
thieves and bandits; but the sheep did not listen to them. I am the gate.
Whoever enters by me will be saved, and will come in and go out and
find pasture.... I am the good shepherd. I know my own and my own
know me, just as the Father knows me and I know the Father. And I
lay down my life for the sheep."   — JOHN 10:3-5, 7-9, 14-15

4. DEATH IS THE BEGINNING

HE WILL COME TO take us in His arms and give us the kiss of
peace.... Thus, we shall end our life in the holy kiss of the Lord,
an admirable kiss of divine condescension by which, according
to St. Bernard, it is not a matter of approaching face-to-face and
mouth-to-mouth. Rather, it means that the Creator draws close
to His creature, and man and God are united for all eternity.

Hand over to Him your departure and the departure of others from this earth, when, where, and as He wills.

O death, I do not know who can fear you, for through you
life begins!

For this perishable body must put on imperishability, and this mortal body must put on immortality. When this perishable body puts on imperishability, and this mortal body puts on immortality, then the saying that is written will be fulfilled:

"Death has been swallowed up in victory."
"Where, O death, is your victory?
Where, O death, is your sting?"

— 1 CORINTHIANS 15:53-55

5. FOOLISH PEOPLE

How BEAUTIFUL ARE THE souls in whom the heavenly Spouse reigns. If all were to be shown this beauty, we should certainly not see so many of our foolish brethren hastening to where God is not to be found.

May God protect us, as He has always done, from identifying ourselves with these foolish ones, according to heavenly Wisdom.

Therefore, always be faithful to God in observing the promises you made Him, and pay no attention to the mocking of the foolish. Know that the saints were always mocked by the world and the worldly, but even so, they placed the world and its maxims under their feet.

Do not let the persecution of worldly people, and of all those who live without the Spirit of Jesus Christ, deter you from following the road trodden by the saints.

So do not be foolish, but understand what the will of the Lord is.

— EPHESIANS 5:17

6. LOVE YOUR NEIGHBOR

FOR ONE WHO IS inflamed with divine love, helping a neighbor in need is a fever which consumes him by degrees. And he would give his life a thousand times if he could induce a soul to offer one more act of praise to the Lord.

Holiness means loving our neighbor as ourselves for love of God. In this connection, holiness means loving those who curse us, who hate and persecute us, and even doing good to them.

Treat your neighbor well and don't get angry. When necessary, say these words of the divine Master: "I love my neighbors, oh, Eternal Father, because You love them, and You gave them to me as brothers and sisters, and You want me to love them as you do."

The commandments, "You shall not commit adultery; You shall not murder; You shall not steal; You shall not covet"; and any other commandment, are summed up in this word, "Love your neighbor as yourself." Love does no wrong to a neighbor; therefore, love is the fulfilling of the law. — ROMANS 13:9-10

7. GUARDIAN OF YOUR SOUL

INTO THE DEEPEST PART of the soul no one has the power to enter except God, not even the good spirits.

I know it is only Jesus who probes the depths of your soul; only Jesus has a full knowledge of your desires and needs.... Jesus is with you; He is yours, and nobody can dispute this.

For you were going astray like sheep, but now you have returned to the shepherd and guardian of your souls. — 1 PETER 2:25

8. UNEASINESS AND USELESS ANXIETY

WE SHOULD BE ON the alert for every slightest sign of uneasiness, and as soon as we realize we have fallen into dejection, we must turn to God with filial confidence and abandon ourselves completely to Him. All unrest on our part is displeasing to Jesus, since such uneasiness is never unaccompanied by imperfection and can always be traced to egotism and self-love. The soul must be saddened by one thing alone: offending God, and even in this we must be very cautious. We must be sorry, it is true, for our failings, but with a calm sorrow, while we continue to trust in divine Mercy.... I beg you to set aside these excessive and useless anxieties. The Lord is with you, and there is no room for fear.

Cast all your anxiety on him, because he cares for you.

— 1 PETER 5:7

9. PIETY AND ZEAL LIKE ST. CLARE AND ST. FRANCIS

LET US ALSO ASK our good Jesus for the humility, trust, and faith of our dear St. Clare; let us pray fervently to Jesus like her. Let us abandon ourselves to Him, detaching ourselves from this lying world where everything is folly and vanity; where everything passes and only God remains to the soul, if it knows how to love Him well. Those souls who throw themselves into the whirlpool of worldly preoccupations are poor and unfortunate. The more they love the world, the more their passions multiply, the more their desires are lit, the more they find themselves incapable of carrying out their projects, and thus they are uneasy, impatient, affected by that shock that breaks their hearts; those hearts which do not beat with charity and holy love. Let us pray for these unfortunate and miserable souls, that Jesus may forgive them and draw them to Himself in His infinite mercy. You who have received many gifts and graces from Jesus, continue to increase always in the life of virtue, and your piety and zeal will recall those who are far from the right path, and thus you will praise the Lord, along with our common father St. Francis of Assisi, in all the works of creation, obtaining copious rewards on earth and in heaven.

Do not lag in zeal, be ardent in spirit, serve the Lord. Rejoice in hope, be patient in suffering, persevere in prayer. Contribute to the needs of the saints; extend hospitality to strangers. — ROMANS 12:11-13

10. SOLITUDE AND SILENCE

I OFTEN THINK THAT THERE is only one thing in this base world which can soothe the most acute pain which pierces the heart when we see ourselves far from God, the source and consolation of distressed souls. That one thing is solitude, for here the soul enjoys sweet rest in the One who is its true peace.

I want the heavenly Father to grant you the grace of stability in all your resolutions, not least of all your resolution to grow in holiness and to be silent and reduce to silence everything around you, so that you may hear the divine voice of the Beloved and establish with Him a tranquil and everlasting dialogue.

Recollect yourself continually, and may your whole life be hidden in Jesus and with Jesus in the Garden of Gethsemane, that is to say, in the silence of meditation and prayer.

Try to be always more docile to grace and more and more generous with Jesus, making absolutely everything around you and within you to be silent. Don't worry; rest trustfully in the arms of divine Mercy.

Silently adore the delicacy of the workings of divine grace.

Be silent before the Lord GOD! — ZEPHANIAH 1:7

11. LIKE ST. THÉRÈSE

ST. THÉRÈSE OF THE CHILD JESUS used to say, "I don't want to choose either to die or to live, but let Jesus do as He likes with me." I see clearly that this is the image of all souls who are stripped of self and filled with God.... What St. Thérèse has said ought to be said by every soul inflamed with love of God.

"Then I said, 'See, God, I have come to do your will,
O God....'"
... then he added, "See, I have come to do your will."
— HEBREWS 10:7, 9

12. HIS GRACE

PRAISE BE TO GOD who never leaves uncomforted the soul who hopes in Him and abandons itself to Him! ... Even in a soul who is sorely tried, Jesus makes it clear that "my grace is sufficient for you."

The grace that is meted out to you from above is sufficient for you because God's power achieves its purpose by means of our weakness.

May divine grace guard and sustain you in everything.

Therefore, to keep me from being too elated, a thorn was given me in the flesh, a messenger of Satan to torment me, to keep me from being too elated. Three times I appealed to the Lord about this, that it would leave me, but he said to me, "My grace is sufficient for you, for power is made perfect in weakness." — 2 CORINTHIANS 12:7-9

13. IF HE HIDES

BE QUITE SURE THAT all that is going on within your soul is decreed by the Lord, and for this reason you must not be afraid of acting wrongly, in a word, of offending God. If this most tender Spouse hides from your soul, it is not because He intends to punish your infidelity, as you imagine, but because He wants to test more and more your faith and steadfastness and at the same time to purify you of certain little attachments which, to the eyes of the flesh, do not appear as such.

If Jesus manifests Himself, thank Him, and if He remains hidden, thank Him just the same; all is a trick of Love.

> *Truly, you are a God who hides himself,*
> *O God of Israel, the Savior.*
> *All of them are put to shame and confounded,*
> *the makers of idols go in confusion together.*
> *But Israel is saved by the LORD*
> *with everlasting salvation;*
> *you shall not be put to shame or confounded*
> *to all eternity.* — ISAIAH 45:15-17

14. THE LIGHT

THE DARKNESS IN YOUR soul is light; in fact, it is the very Sun of Justice that is shining in your soul. This is the truth and the whole truth.

What does it matter if you don't see the light? Indeed, you mustn't see it, but the light is there all the same. It is within you, and one day you will see it.

In the beginning was the Word, and the Word was with God, and the Word was God. He was in the beginning with God. All things came into being through him, and without him not one thing came into being. What has come into being in him was life, and the life was the light of all people. The light shines in the darkness, and the darkness did not overcome it. — JOHN 1:1-5

15. PILOT OF YOUR SOUL

I BEG YOU NOT TO worry about your own soul. Jesus loves you all the time, and when Jesus loves, what is there to fear? Be careful all the time not to let your occupations upset your spiritual life and cause you anxiety, and although you set out over the waves and against the wind of many perplexities, keep your gaze fixed upward and say to Our Lord continually, "Dear God, I am rowing and sailing for You; be my Pilot and my Oarsman." Have no fear of anything; be consoled, for when you reach heaven, the delights you will enjoy will compensate you for the hardships endured in getting there.

O Lord God of hosts,
who is as mighty as you, O Lord?
Your faithfulness surrounds you.
You rule the raging of the sea;
when its waves rise, you still them.   — Psalm 89:8-9

16. Closer, Lord

Always keep your soul situated in the presence of God, while
you go about your exterior practices, and let your soul be cheerful and active when practicing interior prayers, just like the bees
that do not fly within their hives when they go about their
work, but only fly when they leave it.

At all events, let us always stir up our faith and exclaim with
the humble and patient Job, "Set me closer to you, Lord, that I
may feel your presence, then let all hell be turned loose on me,
and I will have no fear" [see Job 14:13; 17:3].

He said, "My presence will go with you, and I will give you rest." And
he said to him, "If your presence will not go, do not carry us up from
here. For how shall it be known that I have found favor in your sight, I
and your people, unless you go with us? In this way, we shall be distinct,
I and your people, from every people on the face of the earth."

The LORD said to Moses, "I will do the very thing that you have asked; for you have found favor in my sight, and I know you by name."

— EXODUS 33:14–17

17. DIVINE CRAFTSMAN

YOU COMPLAIN BECAUSE THE same trials are constantly returning. But look here; what have you to fear? Are you afraid of the divine Craftsman who wants to perfect His masterpiece in this way? Would you like to come from the hands of such a magnificent Artist as a mere sketch and no more? Yet you yourself like to produce perfect works! I laugh and laugh loudly at the manner in which God treats you. Listen; just keep cheerful, be at peace, and let God do as He pleases. None of the things you fear will come to pass. Time will justify my words.

I exhort you not to doubt divine pleasure in your regard. Confide, therefore, in God; always humble yourself more and more under the hand of the divine Craftsman, and let yourself be guided as He pleases.

Yet, O LORD, you are our Father;
we are the clay, and you are our potter;
we are all the work of your hand.

— ISAIAH 64:8

18. SUCCESS OR NOT

IF GOD GRANTS YOU success, then bless Him; if He does not choose to grant it, bless Him just the same. It should be sufficient for you to have striven to succeed. The Lord — and even reason itself — demands not the results but the effort we make, the necessary commitment and diligence. This depends on us, while success does not.

Fear nothing; Jesus is and always will be totally yours, and nobody will take Him from you. Do not allow yourself to be overcome by discouragement if you don't always visibly see your every effort crowned. Jesus sees, rewards, and commands goodwill and not good success, because the latter does not depend on human effort and work.

So continue to do good, and leave the good outcome to Jesus.

Then I replied to them, "The God of heaven is the one who will give us success, and we his servants are going to start building...."

— NEHEMIAH 2:20

19. NO OFFENSE TO GOD

SCRIPTURE ASSURES US THAT combat is an undeniable sign of the soul's union with God and a token of His Presence in the depths of that soul. Let this assurance and this thought console you, and take courage from the example of the divine Master, of whom it is written that He was "in every respect tempted as we are, yet without sinning" [Hebrews 4:15]. He was tempted and tried to the point where He could no longer bear it and cried out, "My God, my God, why have you forsaken me?" [Psalm 22:1; Matthew 27:46] ... In point of fact, when the soul grieves and fears to offend God, it doesn't offend Him and is very far from doing so.

Some people think they are offending God when they feel a violent interior inclination to evil. Take heart, you chosen soul, for in this there is no sin, since the holy apostle himself, a chosen instrument, experienced this dreadful conflict within him: "When I intend to do good," he says, "I find within me a power which inclines me to evil" [Romans 7:21]. Even when carnal impulses are violently felt, there can be no sin when the will does not consent to them.

The soul that fears offending God and has the sincere desire not to do so, but to love Him, does not offend Him, in fact, but loves Him.

For I delight in the law of God in my inmost self, but I see in my members another law at war with the law of my mind, making me captive to the law of sin that dwells in my members. Wretched man that I am! Who will rescue me from this body of death? Thanks be to God through Jesus Christ our Lord! ... For the law of the Spirit of life in Christ Jesus has set you free from the law of sin and of death.

— ROMANS 7:22–25, 8:2

20. YOUR *FIAT*, YOUR *LET IT BE DONE*

O HOW SWEET AND YET how bitter is this "May God's will be done." It cuts and heals, it wounds and cures; it deals death, and at the same time gives life. O sweet torments, why are you so unbearable and so lovable simultaneously? O sweet wounds, why is it that, although so painful, you apply balm to the soul and, at the same time, prepare it to submit to the blows of fresh trials?

Fiat — let it be done! We must abandon life and everything we are, leaving it at the disposition of divine Providence, given that we do not live and do not belong to ourselves but to [Him] who, in order to render us His, desired to make us entirely His in such a loving manner.

Fiat voluntas Dei — God's will be done!

Then Mary said, "Here am I, the servant of the Lord; let it be with me according to your word." — LUKE 1:38

21. UTTERLY GOD'S

CONTINUE TO LIVE ENTIRELY in God in the midst of the trials to which His goodness exposes you. What great happiness it is to be utterly in God, since He loves His own, protects and guides them, and leads them to the haven of eternity for which they long! Remain like this, therefore, and never allow your soul to become sad, to be grieved, or to entertain scruples, for the One who has loved it and died to give it life is tender and good and lovable. This great God has willed that you be all His. He has made you desire this, and you have followed Him; He has enabled you to avail of the true means to correspond to His divine call. Now, without a doubt, you are His.

Because of the exultation of possessing Him within me, I cannot refrain from saying with the most holy Virgin, "My spirit rejoices in God my Savior" [Luke 1:47]. Possessing Him within me, I am impelled to say with the spouse of the sacred Song, "I found him whom my soul loves; I held him and would not let him go" [Song of Solomon 3:4].

Meanwhile, live joyfully in God and for God.

My beloved is mine and I am his;
he pastures his flock among the lilies.

— SONG OF SOLOMON 2:16

22. YOUR IMPERFECTIONS

BE PATIENT IN BEARING your imperfections, if you hold your perfection dear. Remember that this is a very important matter for the building of your spiritual structure. If you want this structure to be masterfully and quickly erected, try to patiently bear your imperfections.

... We must see that even our imperfections die little by little. "Oh, happy imperfections!" we can exclaim. They enable us to become aware of our great misery; they exercise us in humility, causing us to despise ourselves; and they exercise us in patience and diligence. And in spite of our imperfections, God observes the readiness of our hearts, which is perfect.

Therefore, my friends, since we have confidence to enter the sanctuary by the blood of Jesus, by the new and living way that he opened for us through the curtain (that is, through his flesh), and since we have a great priest over the house of God, let us approach with a true heart in full assurance of faith, with our hearts sprinkled clean from an evil conscience and our bodies washed with pure water. — HEBREWS 10:19-22

23. Victory Will Smile on You

IN THE COMBAT, there is a crown to be won, and the better the fight put up by the soul, the more numerous the palms of victory. Don't you know how the apostle St. James exhorted his brethren to rejoice when they were harassed by various storms and numerous reverses? "Count it all joy, my brethren, when you meet various trials" [James 1:2].

May divine Mercy see to it that your prayers are granted ... and give you total victory over the enemy whom you should not fear at all, because God, who is faithful to His promises, will not permit you to be oppressed.

Courage, then, for Jesus is with you, and victory will certainly smile on you.

The LORD, your God, is in your midst,
*   a warrior who gives victory;*
he will rejoice over you with gladness,
*   he will renew you in his love;*
he will exult over you with loud singing
*   as on a day of festival.*   — ZEPHANIAH 3:17-18

24. YOUR CALLING AND MINISTRY

ALL OF US ARE not called by God to save souls and promote His glory by the noble ministry of preaching. Remember, moreover, that this is not the only means of achieving these two great ideals. You can promote God's glory and work for the salvation of souls by means of a truly Christian life, by praying without ceasing that "His kingdom come," that His name "be hallowed," that "we may not be led into temptation," and that He "deliver us from evil" [Luke 11:2-4]. This is what you ought to do, offering yourself continually to the Lord for this purpose. Pray ... pray ... pray.... I exhort you once more to devote yourself entirely — and induce as many others as you can to devote themselves — to the ends I have already explained to you. You may be perfectly sure that this is the highest form of ministry that anyone can carry on in the church of God. Abide resolutely by this statement of mine, which is precisely what Jesus tells us, and treat with contempt all the suggestions to the contrary which the devil proposes to you.

Then Jesus told them a parable about their need to pray always and not to lose heart.... "And will not God grant justice to his chosen ones who cry to him day and night? Will he delay long in helping them? I tell you, he will quickly grant justice to them." — LUKE 18:1, 7-8

25. PHYSICIAN OF SOULS

THE SOUL THAT IS destined to reign with Jesus Christ in eternal glory must be remodeled by the blows of hammer and chisel. But what are these blows of hammer and chisel by which the divine Artist prepares the stone, that is to say, the chosen soul? These strokes of the chisel are the shadows, fears, temptations, spiritual torments, and agitation — with a dash of desolation and even of physical pain. Thank the infinite mercy of the eternal Father, then, for treating your soul in this way, for you are destined to be saved. What I say is, why not rejoice at this loving treatment by the best of all fathers? Open your heart to this heavenly Physician of souls and abandon yourself with complete confidence in His most holy embrace. He is treating you as one chosen to follow Jesus closely up the hill of Calvary.

"You did not choose me but I chose you." — JOHN 15:16

26. SHELTER IN HIS HEART

YOU SEE YOURSELF IN tribulation, and God repeats to you through the mouth of authority, "I will be with him in trouble"

[Psalm 91:15]. You believe you are abandoned, but I assure you that Jesus is holding you more tightly than ever to His divine Heart.

Continue calmly, and rest upon this divine Heart without the slightest fear, because there you are well sheltered from the storm, and not even God's justice can reach you.

It will serve as a pavilion, a shade by day from the heat, and a refuge and a shelter from the storm and rain. — Isaiah 4:6

27. A Different Kind of Love

You are trying to measure, understand, feel, and touch this love which you have for God, but you must accept as certain that the more you love God, the less you feel this love. This seems too strange and impossible in the case of transient love for creatures in this poor world, but when it is a case of love for the Spouse of your soul, things are very different. I am not able to explain this truth very clearly, but you can take it as certain that the matter is as I have said. God is incomprehensible and inaccessible; hence, the more you penetrate into the love of this Supreme Good, the more the sentiment of love toward Him — which is beyond your soul's knowledge — seems to diminish, until you consider that you no longer love Him at all. In fact, in certain instances it seems to you that this is really the case, but events prove the very opposite. That continual fear of losing your God, that holy circumspection which makes you look carefully where to place your feet so as not to stumble, that courage in facing the assaults of the enemy, that resignation to God's kingdom established in your own heart and in the hearts of others, are the clearest proofs of your soul's love for the Supreme Good.

I pray that you may have the power to comprehend, with all the saints, what is the breadth and length and height and depth, and to know the love of Christ that surpasses knowledge, so that you may be filled with all the fullness of God. — EPHESIANS 3:18-19

28. LIFE WELL SPENT

YOU CAN NEVER TAKE too much trouble for the sanctification of a soul.

Would you not give your life a thousand times rather than resolve to go against God's will? You are quite sure of this, and you feel it in your heart. Let this, then, be the touchstone by which you recognize and convince yourself that your life is well spent.... Time spent for God's glory and the salvation of souls must never be regretted, for it is never badly spent. Don't worry, therefore.

My brothers and sisters, if anyone among you wanders from the truth and is brought back by another, you should know that whoever brings back a sinner from wandering will save the sinner's soul from death and will cover a multitude of sins. — JAMES 5:19-20

29. SCRIPTURE AND OTHER HOLY BOOKS

HELP YOURSELF BY READING holy books. I earnestly desire to see you reading such books at all times, for this reading provides excellent food for the soul and conduces to great progress along the path of perfection, by no means inferior to what we obtain through prayer and holy meditation. In prayer and meditation, it is we ourselves who speak to the Lord, while in holy reading it is God who speaks to us. Try to treasure these holy readings as much as you can and you will very soon be aware of a spiritual renewal within you. Before beginning to read these books, raise your mind to the Lord and implore Him to guide your mind, to speak to your heart and move your will. But this is not sufficient. It is also advisable, before you start to read, and from time to time in the course of your reading, to declare before the Lord that you are not reading for the purpose of study or to satisfy your curiosity, but solely to give Him pleasure and enjoyment.

But as for you, continue in what you have learned and firmly believed, knowing from whom you learned it, and how from childhood you have known the sacred writings that are able to instruct you for salvation through faith in Christ Jesus. All scripture is inspired by God and is useful for teaching, for reproof, for correction, and for training in righteousness, so that everyone who belongs to God may be proficient, equipped for every good work.   — 2 TIMOTHY 3:14-17

30. NOT CRUSHED

ALL SOULS WHO LOVE Jesus must be tried by the fires of temptation. St. Paul himself experienced this very harsh trial during his pilgrimage, so that with groans and anguish he incessantly asked to be freed from it, but Jesus replied that His grace would be enough [see 2 Corinthians 12:9]. God allows the same voice to be heard by all souls who want to love Him with sincerity and purity of heart. How can we doubt this? Isn't our God faithful beyond all human concepts, so that He would not permit us to be tempted beyond our strength [see 1 Corinthians 10:13]?

You say, "But Paul was a saint; he was filled with the Holy Spirit and therefore had nothing to fear, while I, on the other hand, see myself weak and exhausted in spirit, which is precisely the reason why I fear to be overcome." Has the Lord not told us that He is faithful and that He promises never to allow us to be vanquished? Yes, God is faithful, and He will not let you be tempted beyond your strength, but with the temptation will also provide the way of escape, that you may be able to endure it. How could you persuade yourself of anything else? Isn't our good God far above anything we can conceive? Isn't He more interested than we are in our salvation? How many times has He not given us proof of this? How many victories have you not gained over your very powerful enemies — and over yourself — through the divine assistance, without which you would inevitably have been crushed?

We are afflicted in every way, but not crushed; perplexed, but not driven to despair; persecuted, but not forsaken; struck down, but not destroyed; always carrying in the body the death of Jesus, so that the life of Jesus may also be made visible in our bodies.

— 2 Corinthians 4:8-10

31. Fix Your Gaze

In order that we may willingly accept the tribulations lavished on us by the divine Mercy, let us keep our gaze fixed on the heavenly home reserved for us; let us constantly contemplate it and aim at it with the greatest care.... Enchanted by these eternal delights, our minds distinguish what is valuable from what is worthless. As for ourselves who have been called through the goodness of the Most High God to reign with the divine Bridegroom, whose minds are enlightened by God's true light, let us fix our gaze constantly on the splendor of the heavenly Jerusalem. Let the consideration of all those good things to be possessed in that realm provide us with delightful food for our thought.

And I heard a loud voice from the throne saying,
  "See, the home of God is among mortals.
  He will dwell with them;
  they will be his peoples,
  and God himself will be with them;
  he will wipe every tear from their eyes.
  Death will be no more;
  mourning and crying and pain will be no more...."

— REVELATION 21:3–4

32. OVERCOMING DEPRESSION

WHENEVER YOU ARE SEIZED by depression or sadness, let your thoughts dwell on that fateful night on which the Son of God began the work of redemption in the solitude of Gethsemane, and offer your own sufferings to the divine Father, along with the sufferings of Jesus. You must also have recourse to some good reading and avoid those distressing readings which are not suitable for you. If, after all this, you still feel depressed, then apply yourself to some manual work or something else which distracts you. You might even start singing some cheerful song and, if possible, invite others to sing with you. I also want you to talk about this with your loved ones. Don't worry, for all will work out for the triumph of God's glory.

You are loved by Jesus, and Jesus has already forgiven your sins, so there can be no further reason for your spirit to be depressed. Your desire to convince yourself to the contrary is truly a waste of time; it is an offense to the Heart of this most tender Lover of ours.

Finally, beloved, whatever is true, whatever is honorable, whatever is just, whatever is pure, whatever is pleasing, whatever is commendable, if there is any excellence and if there is anything worthy of praise, think about these things. — PHILIPPIANS 4:8

33. WORK OF THE HOLY SPIRIT

I ASSURE YOU THAT THE distress you still experience in seeing yourself continually exposed to occasions of offending God is entirely the effect of divine grace, which the most merciful Lord has poured abundantly into your heart. All this is a most sure sign that the love which the Holy Spirit has poured into your heart is not dead, but active [see Romans 5:5].

Therefore, live tranquilly and allow yourself to be transported by the Spirit of the Lord, who is working within you in a marvelous manner. Humble yourself more and more, because in this way the Lord will enrich you with more and more favors.

Yes, live tranquilly, because Jesus is with you. Let the Spirit of the Lord blow where and when He wishes.

Do not quench the Spirit. — 1 THESSALONIANS 5:19

34. TO PROGRESS IN HOLINESS

IN THE FIRST PLACE, you must take care never to quarrel with anyone, never to contend with anyone whomsoever. If you act otherwise, it means good-bye to peace and charity. To be inordinately attached to your own opinion is invariably a source and beginning of discord. St. Paul exhorts us to be united in the same mind and the same judgment against this wretched vice. Be on your guard also against boastful vanity, a vice to be found [even] in devout persons. It leads us, without our being aware of the fact, to appear invariably somewhat above others, to gain the esteem of all. St. Paul also warns his dear Philippians against this when he says, "Do nothing from selfishness or conceit" [Philippians 2:3]. This great saint, filled with the Spirit of the Lord, saw clearly and fully the evil that would result for those holy Christians if this wretched vice were to succeed in penetrating into their souls, which is why he warned them.

Do nothing from selfish ambition or conceit, but in humility regard others as better than yourselves. Let each of you look not to your own interests, but to the interests of others. Let the same mind be in you that was in Christ Jesus,

> *who, though he was in the form of God,*
> *did not regard equality with God*
> *as something to be exploited....* — PHILIPPIANS 2:3-6

35. BEAUTY AND SPLENDOR OF SOUL

BY A MOST WISE order and a most singular love, our heavenly Father, in His goodness, makes it impossible for us to remove those bodily deformities which we inherit from nature, our mother. If we were to give a lot of thought to — and waste much time and effort in — trying to correct our superficial bodily defects, even in arranging our hair so that not even a single strand was out of place, tell me, what would we not do to rectify and drive far from us the physical deformities we bear in our bodies? Unfortunately, we are never done trying to improve our appearance. Indeed, all our efforts are directed toward improving the body and making it more and more beautiful. Less attention is perhaps devoted to the soul, which we may have treated as a negligible quantity.... The soul's cooperation with divine grace is all that is required to enable it to develop, to reach such a degree of splendor and beauty, as to attract, not so much the loving and astonished gaze of the angels, but the gaze of God Himself.

May the God of peace himself sanctify you entirely; and may your spirit and soul and body be kept sound and blameless at the coming of our Lord Jesus Christ. The one who calls you is faithful, and he will do this.

— 1 THESSALONIANS 5:23-24

36. TWO-FOLD LIFE

WE HAVE A TWO-FOLD LIFE. We have a natural life received from Adam through procreation and which is therefore an earthly and corruptible life filled with base passions and love of self. The other life is a supernatural one received from Jesus at baptism and therefore a spiritual, heavenly life by which we practice virtue.... The Christian who has forgotten his true vocation and is merely a Christian in name, a worldly Christian, judges things differently. His judgment is the exact opposite of that of the Christian worthy of the name who lives according to the Spirit of Jesus Christ. The former judges material things based on their capacity to satisfy his vanity and his passions. The latter, on the other hand, invariably judges them in relation to eternal things. Hence, the one that is a Christian merely in name, the Christian in high society, sets a great value on honors, wealth, fleeting things, comforts, and all that this wretched world has to offer. Oh, foolish one, enter into yourself and remember that by your baptism you renounced the world and are dead to it.

So if you have been raised with Christ, seek the things that are above, where Christ is, seated at the right hand of God. Set your minds on things that are above, not on things that are on earth, for you have died, and your life is hidden with Christ in God. When Christ who is your life is revealed, then you also will be revealed with him in glory.

— COLOSSIANS 3:1-4

37. SLOW TO ANGER

THE VICES WHICH LEAD us to offend our neighbor by interior acts, according to St. Paul, are anger, wrath, and malice [see Colossians 3:8]. Anger is a moral passion, which also exists in good people, and in itself is not sinful. But if we do not know how to control it, it becomes sinful, as happens when we are angry with someone who does not deserve it; or before we have reason to be angry; or in matters which do not justify our anger. The apostle warns us to refrain from these types of anger.

You must understand this, my beloved: let everyone be quick to listen, slow to speak, slow to anger; for your anger does not produce God's righteousness. Therefore rid yourselves of all sordidness and rank growth of wickedness, and welcome with meekness the implanted word that has the power to save your souls. — JAMES 1:19-21

38. ON THE CROSS WITH JESUS

LET US FOLLOW THE divine Master up the steep slope of Calvary loaded with our cross; and when it pleases Him to place us on the cross by confining us to a bed of sickness, let us thank Him and consider ourselves lucky to be honored in this way, aware that to be on the cross with Jesus is infinitely more perfect than merely contemplating Jesus Himself on the cross.

Oh, how sublime and sweet is the divine Master's delightful invitation, "If any would come after me, let him deny himself and take up his cross and follow me" [Matthew 16:24]. It was this invitation which caused St. Teresa to come out with that prayer to the divine Bridegroom, "Either to suffer or to die." It was this same invitation which made St. Mary Magdalen de' Pazzi utter the words, "Always to suffer and never to die." It was this invitation also which caused our seraphic father, St. Francis of Assisi, caught up in ecstasy, to exclaim, "So much good awaits me that every suffering is a joy."

Live for [Him] who died for us, and be crucified along with Him.

I have been crucified with Christ; and it is no longer I who live, but it is Christ who lives in me. And the life I now live in the flesh I live by faith in the Son of God, who loved me and gave himself for me.

— GALATIANS 2:19-20

39. KEEP RUNNING

I BESEECH YOU, by the meekness of Jesus and by the bowels of mercy of the heavenly Father, never to slacken on the path of virtue. Keep on running and don't ever make up your mind to stop, for you know that to stand still on this path is equivalent to retracing your steps.

Run then, without growing weary, and may the Lord direct and guide your steps so that you may not fall. Make haste, I tell you, for the road is long and time is very short. Run; let us all run, so that at the end of our journey we may say with the holy apostle, "I have finished the race, I have kept the faith" [2 Timothy 4:7].

As for me, I am already being poured out as a libation, and the time of my departure has come. I have fought the good fight, I have finished the race, I have kept the faith. From now on there is reserved for me the crown of righteousness, which the Lord, the righteous judge, will give me on that day, and not only to me but also to all who have longed for his appearing. — 2 TIMOTHY 4:6–8

40. FEWER COMPLAINTS, PLEASE

IS IT POSSIBLE THAT you are never satisfied with yourself? Jesus loves you with a loving partiality in spite of all your unworthiness. He sends down a torrent of graces upon you, and yet you complain. It is about time this ended and you convinced yourself that you are greatly in the Lord's debt. Hence, less complaints, more gratitude, and a great deal of thanksgiving. You ought to ask Our Lord for just one thing: to love Him. All the rest should be thanksgiving.

And let the peace of Christ rule in your hearts, to which indeed you were called in the one body. And be thankful. Let the word of Christ dwell

*in you richly; teach and admonish one another in all wisdom; and with
gratitude in your hearts sing psalms, hymns, and spiritual songs to God.
And whatever you do, in word or deed, do everything in the name of the
Lord Jesus, giving thanks to God the Father through him.*

— COLOSSIANS 3:15-17

41. ALL GOOD IN YOU

I MYSELF CANNOT SEE HOW a person can become proud on account of the gifts he recognizes in himself. It seems to me that
the richer he sees himself to be, the more reason he has to humble himself before the Lord, for the Lord's gifts increase and he
can never fully repay the Giver of all good things. As for you,
what have you in particular to be proud of? What do you have
that you did not receive? If then you received all, why do you
boast as if it were your own? Oh, whenever the tempter wants
you to be puffed up with pride, say to yourself, "All that is good
in me I have received from God on loan, and I should be a fool
to boast of what is not mine." Act in this way and have no fear.

*What do you have that you did not receive? And if you received it, why
do you boast as if it were not a gift?* — I CORINTHIANS 4:7

42. LOVING FATHER

OH, OPEN YOUR HEART to the Father, the most loving of all fathers, and let Him act freely within you. Let us not be stingy with One who enriches us even too much, whose generosity is endless and knows no limits. Your only thought should be to love God and to grow more and more in virtue and in holy love, which is the bond of Christian perfection.

The Lord is a Father, the most tender and best of fathers. He cannot fail to be moved when his children appeal to Him.

The Lord is with you, not as a judge but as a loving Father, a beloved Spouse. He is with you — patient, suffering, eager — when you are crushed, trampled upon, heartbroken, in the shadows of the night, and even more so in the desolation of Gethsemane. He is associated with you in your suffering and has associated you in His own. This is the whole fact of the matter; this is the truth and the only truth.

"On that day you will know that I am in my Father, and you in me, and I in you. They who have my commandments and keep them are those who love me; and those who love me will be loved by my Father, and I will love them and reveal myself to them." — JOHN 14:20-21

43. OBTAIN THE PRIZE

ESPECIALLY IN THE THINGS that are hardest for you, do not be in a hurry to escape from them. Raise your heart to the divine Father more than ever on these occasions and say to Him, "Lord, God of my heart, You alone know and read all my troubles. You alone are aware that all my distress springs from my fear of losing You; of offending You; from my fear of not loving You as much as I should — and desire — to love You. If You, to whom everything is present and who alone can read the future, know that it is for Your greater glory and for my salvation that I should remain in this state, then let it be so. I don't want to escape from it. Give me the strength to fight and to obtain the prize due to strong souls."

Not that I have already obtained this or have already reached the goal; but I press on to make it my own, because Christ Jesus has made me his own. Beloved, I do not consider that I have made it my own; but this one thing I do: forgetting what lies behind and straining forward to what lies ahead, I press on toward the goal for the prize of the heavenly call of God in Christ Jesus. — PHILIPPIANS 3:12-14

44. HERE IS CHRIST

LIVE IN SUCH A way that the heavenly Father may be proud of you, as He is proud of so many other chosen souls like your own. Live in such a way that you may be able to repeat at every moment with the apostle St. Paul, "Be imitators of me, as I am of Jesus Christ" [1 Corinthians 4:16]. Live in such a way, I repeat, that the world will be forced to say of you, "Here is Christ." Oh, for pity's sake, do not consider this an exaggeration! Every Christian who is a true imitator and follower of the fair Nazarene can — and must — call himself a "second Christ" and show forth most clearly in his life the entire image of Christ. Oh, if only all Christians were to live up to their vocation, this very land of exile would be changed into a paradise.

May Jesus always be the life of your heart, sustaining it in all trials and transforming it into His very self.

Be imitators of me, as I am of Christ. — 1 CORINTHIANS 11:1

45. Our Enemies Are God's Enemies Too

Let us remember that if they are our enemies, they are also God's enemies. Well, then, the enemies of God insult the cross and all those who are crucified upon it with the Son of God. For you, this ought to be a source of gladness, as it is for many souls.

Brothers and sisters, join in imitating me, and observe those who live according to the example you have in us. For many live as enemies of the cross of Christ; I have often told you of them, and now I tell you even with tears. Their end is destruction; their god is the belly; and their glory is in their shame; their minds are set on earthly things. But our citizenship is in heaven, and it is from there that we are expecting a Savior, the Lord Jesus Christ. — Philippians 3:17–20

46. Need More?

Say to Jesus, "Do you want great love from me, Jesus? I, too, desire this, just as a deer longs to reach a flowing stream, but as You see, I have no more love to give [see Psalm 42:1]. Give me some more love, and I'll offer it to You!" Do not doubt that Jesus, who is so good, will accept your offer; so be at peace.

"Ask, and it will be given you; search, and you will find; knock, and the door will be opened for you. For everyone who asks receives, and everyone who searches finds, and for everyone who knocks, the door will be opened." — MATTHEW 7:7-8

47. DEMANDS OF NATURE

IF YOUR BODY SUFFERS and demands its rights, this is a condition of man's life as a wayfarer. Secretly and silently he feels the pain of suffering and naturally wants to escape from it, for man was created to enjoy happiness, and his trials are a consequence of sin. As long as we remain in this world, we shall always feel a natural aversion [to] suffering. This is a chain that will accompany us everywhere. You may be quite sure that if in the higher part, at the apex of our soul, we desire the cross and therefore embrace and submit to it for love of God, this will not prevent us from feeling in the lower part of the soul the demands of nature, which object to suffering. In point of fact, who more than our divine Master loved the cross? But, then, consider that even Christ, in His most-holy humanity, prayed during His voluntary agony that the chalice might pass from Him, if possible. You must agree with me that your own spirit is always willing to do God's will and makes every effort to do it. It is the flesh, on the other hand, that is weak; but God wants the spirit and not the flesh. Let nature object, then, for this feeling does not depend on the will, and therefore it does not make us guilty before God. Rather does it become a cause of merit for us, if we hold it in check and subdue it.

Then he said to them, "I am deeply grieved, even to death; remain here, and stay awake with me." And going a little farther, he threw himself on the ground and prayed, "My Father, if it is possible, let this cup pass from me; yet not what I want but what you want."

— MATTHEW 26:38–39

48. IN ATONEMENT

LET US PRAY INCESSANTLY, and let us suffer according to the divine will. Let us pray and suffer in atonement for our own sins and for those of others.

You are suffering, but believe also that Jesus is suffering in you, for you, and with you. He is associating you in His Passion, and you, as a victim, must make up for your brothers and sisters that which is lacking in the Passion of Jesus Christ. Let the thought that you are not alone in that agony, but rather in good company, be of comfort to you.

I am now rejoicing in my sufferings for your sake, and in my flesh I am completing what is lacking in Christ's afflictions for the sake of his body, that is, the church. — COLOSSIANS 1:24

49. JESUS AS HELMSMAN, AND MARY AS BEACON AND STAR

DO NOT FEAR THE enemy; he will not launch anything against the little ship of your spirit because Jesus is the Helmsman and Mary is the star.

Could this be the end of the trial? Let us hope for this from the mercy of the Lord and the maternal Heart of Mary who can receive everything from the Most High. More than ever, in these days, we should pester the Heart of the Son and that of the Mother....

Have no fear, for you will not be submerged. The little vessel, which is your soul, always possesses the strong anchor of trust in the divine Goodness. This mystical vessel will always have Jesus as Helmsman and Mary as its beacon. Hence, there is no room for fear.

"Do not fear, only believe." — MARK 5:36

50. The Beauty of His Wounds

Jesus glorified is beautiful; but even though He is beautiful in that state, He seems to me to be even more beautiful crucified.

How can a soul, considering Jesus crucified for it, love anything besides Him?

But Thomas (who was called the Twin), one of the twelve, was not with them when Jesus came. So the other disciples told him, "We have seen the Lord." But he said to them, "Unless I see the mark of the nails in his hands, and put my finger in the mark of the nails and my hand in his side, I will not believe."

A week later his disciples were again in the house, and Thomas was with them. Although the doors were shut, Jesus came and stood among them and said, "Peace be with you." Then he said to Thomas, "Put your finger here and see my hands. Reach out your hand and put it in my side. Do not doubt but believe." Thomas answered him, "My Lord and my God!" Jesus said to him, "Have you believed because you have seen me? Blessed are those who have not seen and yet have come to believe."

— John 20:24-29

51. PRAY CONSTANTLY

PRAY CONSTANTLY AND YOU will thus win the victory over your enemies.

I urge you to pray continually to the heavenly Father that He may always keep you close to His divine Heart; that He may make you hear His loving voice more and more clearly; and that He may lead you to correspond with increasing gratitude. Ask Jesus with boundless confidence, like the bride in the Song of Solomon, to draw you after Him and let you smell the fragrance of His anointing oils [see Song of Solomon 1:3-4] so that you may follow swiftly with all the faculties of your soul and body wherever He goes.

Fortify yourself with prayer and wait with a happy soul for the will of God to be accomplished in you.

Let us refer all our actions to Him; let us raise our souls to Him more often. Let us carry out Christian actions more often, along with short prayers. Let us refer everything to God, and let us act and live in Him.

Remember that the only way to gain your health of soul is through prayer; you cannot win the battle without prayer. So the choice is up to you.

Therefore, pray and get others to pray a great deal, so that justice and innocence will triumph.

Pray without ceasing.... — 1 THESSALONIANS 5:17

52. NECESSARY GRATITUDE

ALWAYS GIVE MOST FERVENT thanks to God through Jesus Christ. By so doing, you will prepare yourself very well to receive other favors from heaven. On the other hand, whoever does not appreciate the favors he has already received is very naturally unworthy of further favors.

O give thanks to the LORD, call on his name,
make known his deeds among the peoples.
Sing to him, sing praises to him,
tell of all his wonderful works. — 1 CHRONICLES 16:8-9

53. PATIENT ENDURANCE

BY OUR PERSEVERANCE IN good works, by our patience in fighting the good fight, we shall overcome the insolence of all our enemies. As the Holy Spirit has said, "By your endurance you will gain your lives, for trials produce patience and patience brings testing and from the testing springs hope" [see James 1:2-3].

We must be resigned and patient with ourselves, and in our patience we will possess our souls, as the divine Master tells us [see Luke 21:19].... Say to Him, in a spirit of confidence and humility, "Lord, have mercy, because I am a poor weakling." Then get up in peace, and with a tranquil and serene soul, and with holy indifference, go about your tasks.

As for what fell among the thorns, these are the ones who hear; but as they go on their way, they are choked by the cares and riches and pleasures of life, and their fruit does not mature. But as for that in the good soil, these are the ones who, when they hear the word, hold it fast in an honest and good heart, and bear fruit with patient endurance.

— LUKE 8:14-15

54. NONVIOLENCE WINS

AS WE HAVE SEEN, the victory of Gideon and the Israelites over the Midianites was not gained by the use of arms, but by a singular stratagem of war.... At a sign from the leader, the water jars were smashed and the trumpets blared, while after every trumpet blast the war cry went up, "For the LORD and for

Gideon" [Judges 7:20].... Well then, we, too, have to sustain a very hard fight as long as we live. Let us win this war by that unusual stratagem used by Gideon. Let the light of good works, the strength of the knowledge of God, and the ardent desire for God's Word go before us in this battle. Let us, too, fight to the sound of hymns and psalms and spiritual canticles, by singing and raising our voices loudly to the Lord. Thus will our Lord Jesus make us deserving of the victory, in Him to whom belongs all glory and power, forever and ever.

So Gideon and the hundred who were with him came to the outskirts of the camp at the beginning of the middle watch, when they had just set the watch; and they blew the trumpets and smashed the jars that were in their hands. So the three companies blew the trumpets and broke the jars, holding in their left hands the torches, and in their right hands the trumpets to blow; and they cried, "A sword for the LORD and for Gideon!" Every man stood in his place all around the camp, and all the men in camp ran; they cried out and fled.

— JUDGES 7:19-21

55. PAYMENT FOR HOLY ACTS

THERE IS ONE WHO will repay you two hundredfold for each holy act you perform.

"But love your enemies, do good, and lend, expecting nothing in return. Your reward will be great, and you will be children of the Most High; for he is kind to the ungrateful and the wicked. Be merciful, just as your Father is merciful." — LUKE 6:35-36

56. IN THE SHADOW OF THE DIVINE BRIDEGROOM

DESPISE THE SNARES OF those evil ones, and with boundless trust sit down in the shadow of the divine Bridegroom, fearing nothing. Lucifer's burning rays will not penetrate the shade of such a Tree. Your soul must not fear to be browned by those rays which want to wither it up, for they will make you proceed on your way with ever-greater respect and love. Thus, where the devil would like to harm you, he causes you, instead, to earn new treasures for Paradise. Jesus wants you all for Himself. Stir up your faith, then, and throw yourself with sublime abandonment into the arms of God, and God will carry out the plans He has for you.... Do your very best; then Jesus will perfect this work and be glorified by it.

With great delight I sat in his shadow,
and his fruit was sweet to my taste.

He brought me to the banqueting house,
and his intention toward me was love.

— SONG OF SOLOMON 2:3–4

57. IF GOD IS FOR YOU

I EXHORT YOU, in our most sweet Jesus, never to fear the evil snares of the enemy who tries to make us act dishonorably. Jesus is with you; who can be against you?

So why are you afflicted; what are you afraid of? If God is for you, who could be against you? You become afflicted because God, in His loving goodness, offers you the occasion to gain treasures for heaven. You are afraid because God wants to test the extent of your virtue and fidelity to Him. You are afflicted and afraid because God presents you with the jewels of His only begotten Son, to whom He has promised you as a bride. To be afraid in the arms of the most loving Father, and to be afflicted because He gives you paternal caresses, is purely stupid. Therefore, take heart; with a truly strong and trusting soul, bear the trial God sends you out of loving partiality.

Don't lose heart in the midst of these trials. As long as your heart is faithful to Him, He will not give you more than you can bear. And He will also bear your burdens along with you, when He sees you bending your shoulders, with goodwill, to the cross.

If God is for us, who is against us? He who did not withhold his own Son, but gave him up for all of us, will he not with him also give us everything else? Who will bring any charge against God's elect? It is God who justifies. Who is to condemn? It is Christ Jesus, who died, yes, who was raised, who is at the right hand of God, who indeed intercedes for us. Who will separate us from the love of Christ? ... No, in all these things we are more than conquerors through him who loved us.

— ROMANS 8:31–35, 37

58. TRIUMPH OVER GOD

IN MAN'S STRUGGLE WITH MAN, he fears his enemy, is injured, collapses on the ground, spills blood; there are winners and losers. Whereas where the struggle of man with God is concerned, the contrary takes place. He who trembles before God; he who is oppressed under the weight of tribulation, weighted down at the sight of the deep wounds his sins have made in him; he who rubs his face in the dust; he who lowers himself, humbles himself, cries, shouts, sighs, and prays, it is he who wins, it is he who triumphs.

It is true that God's power triumphs over everything, but humble and suffering prayer triumphs over God Himself! It lowers His arm; extinguishes His lightning; disarms Him; overcomes Him; appeases Him; and makes Him — I would almost say — a friend and dependent.

> *The friendship of the LORD is for those who fear him,*
> *and he makes his covenant known to them.*
> *My eyes are ever toward the LORD,*
> *for he will pluck my feet out of the net.*
>
> — PSALM 25:14-15

59. DIFFICULTIES WHEN DOING GOOD

HOW MANY DIFFICULTIES WE encounter when doing good! But never mind; Jesus will take everything into account. No work done for love of Him will be left without a just reward. Therefore, live tranquilly and resigned to divine will, always keeping present to your mind the fact that our perfection consists in the perfect conformity of our will to that of God. Therefore, let us unite ourselves to it; Jesus will be pleased, and we will sanctify ourselves.

Don't become uneasy if you don't yet succeed in carrying out the acts of virtue as well as you would like, because they do not have a lesser value even when they are done in a weak, heavy, and almost forced manner.

Meanwhile, don't let difficulties you encounter stop you from doing good. Jesus is with you, and you have nothing to fear.

For we are what he has made us, created in Christ Jesus for good works, which God prepared beforehand to be our way of life.

— EPHESIANS 2:10

60. GOD WILL CRUSH THE EVIL ONE

ABOVE ALL, PRAY TO God that you may not be led into temptation.... By behaving thus, even given that Lucifer should sometimes transform himself into an angel of light before you [see 2 Corinthians 11:14], no harm will come to you, so that where the evil one would like you to find death, you will find life.

For while your obedience is known to all, so that I rejoice over you, I want you to be wise in what is good and guileless in what is evil. The God of peace will shortly crush Satan under your feet. The grace of our Lord Jesus Christ be with you. — ROMANS 16:19-20

61. Entirely Pleasing to the Lord

Live entirely for Him, always keeping far from you many useless thoughts, which fill the heart with vanity and confuse and dim the intellect. Be careful to carry out all your actions, even the most insignificant, with the upright intention of pleasing God, casting aside even the slightest thought of self-interest. What greater gain can the soul have than that of pleasing the Lord? Always have a humble idea of yourself, being convinced that any services the soul can render to God, even if they are many, are still of little account. And if they acquire luster and value, it is by the grace of God.

Try to find out what is pleasing to the Lord. Take no part in the unfruitful works of darkness, but instead expose them. For it is shameful even to mention what such people do secretly; but everything exposed by the light becomes visible, for everything that becomes visible is light.

— Ephesians 5:10-14

62. FORGIVENESS IS YOURS

WHEN YOU ARE ASSAILED by fears for what you've done in the past, think of it as lost in the ocean of heavenly Goodness, then turn your mind to the present in which Jesus is with you and loves you. Think of the future, when Jesus will reward your faithfulness and resignation, or rather think of all the graces He has poured out on you and which you certainly have not deliberately abused. Hence, I would ask you in the sweet Lord to cast aside all fear as far as possible — for no one is asked to do what is impossible — and always have confidence, faith, and love. Trust in the Lord, in His forgiveness and protection. Oh yes! You can even rest tranquilly on the bosom of divine Mercy, as a tender little child rests in the arms of its mother.

Your fear of the past is futile, because the goodness of the Lord cancelled and forgot your sins.

> *Surely it was for my welfare*
> *that I had great bitterness;*
> *but you have held back my life*
> *from the pit of destruction,*
> *for you have cast all my sins*
> *behind your back.*

— ISAIAH 38:17

63. YOUR THIRST FOR GOD

How is it possible for the spring of living water flowing from the Heart of God to be far from a soul that runs to it like a thirsty deer [see Psalm 42:1]? But you will retort that you are not satisfied because you feel devoured by an unquenchable thirst, and precisely for this reason you wish to doubt that Jesus is close to you. No, it is not as you would have it. The unquenchable thirst that devours you arises because it has not yet reached the end of its journey; it is not yet totally immersed in the eternal fountain, which cannot take place while we are in a pilgrim state. Woe to the soul when it considers itself satisfied here on earth, because that would be the beginning of its downfall and the soul would be deceived. Be calm; revive your faith, your trust in God.

A Samaritan woman came to draw water, and Jesus said to her, "Give me a drink." (His disciples had gone to the city to buy food.) The Samaritan woman said to him, "How is it that you, a Jew, ask a drink of me, a woman of Samaria?" (Jews do not share things in common with Samaritans.) Jesus answered her, "If you knew the gift of God, and who it is that is saying to you, 'Give me a drink,' you would have asked him, and he would have given you living water." The woman said to him, "Sir, you have no bucket, and the well is deep. Where do you get that living water? Are you greater than our ancestor Jacob, who gave us the well, and with his sons and his flocks drank from it?" Jesus said to her, "Everyone who drinks of this water will be thirsty again, but those who drink of the water that I will give them will never be thirsty. The water that I will give will become in them a spring of water gushing up to eternal life."

— JOHN 4:7-14

64. GOD IS IN THE DARKNESS

LET THE WORLD TURN upside down; let everything be in darkness, in smoke, in turmoil, but God is with you. But if God lives in the darkness and on Mount Sinai amidst the thunder and lightning [see Exodus 19:16], would we not be happy to be close to Him?

I exhort you to love a God crucified amidst the darkness; stay a while with Him. Tell Him, "It does me good to stay here. Let us make three dwellings [see Mark 9:5], one for Our Lord, one for Our Lady, and the other for St. John." Make three crosses anyway; stay at the foot of that of the Son, or that of the Mother, or that of the most beloved disciple. You will be welcomed everywhere.

It was now about noon, and darkness came over the whole land until three in the afternoon, while the sun's light failed; and the curtain of the temple was torn in two. Then Jesus, crying with a loud voice, said, "Father, into your hands I commend my spirit." Having said this, he breathed his last. When the centurion saw what had taken place, he praised God and said, "Certainly this man was innocent." And when all the crowds who had gathered there for this spectacle saw what had taken place, they returned home, beating their breasts. But all his acquaintances, including the women who had followed him from Galilee, stood at a distance, watching these things. — LUKE 23:44-49

65. MAKING PROGRESS

LET US WALK ALWAYS, even with slow steps; as long as we have good intentions we cannot but make progress. No, it is not necessary to be always attentive to everything for the exercise of the virtues. This truly would confuse and muffle your thoughts and affections too much. Have I made myself clear?

Therefore, spin a little every day; draw out your designs until they are finished. But beware of haste, because you would tangle the thread and knot the distaff. Walk always, even if slowly; you will make progress just the same.

So we are always confident; even though we know that while we are at home in the body we are away from the Lord — for we walk by faith, not by sight. Yes, we do have confidence, and we would rather be away from the body and at home with the Lord. So whether we are at home or away, we make it our aim to please him.

— 2 CORINTHIANS 5:6-9

66. YOUR HEART'S RECOURSE

Do NOT BOTHER TOO much to heal your heart, as your efforts would only render it more infirm. Do not try too much to overcome your temptations, as this violence would strengthen them. Despise them, but do not dwell on or become obsessed with them.

Don't fight little temptations with disputes and contestations, but rather, by your heart's merely having recourse to Jesus Crucified, as if you went to kiss His side and feet out of love.

So they left the tomb quickly with fear and great joy, and ran to tell his disciples. Suddenly Jesus met them and said, "Greetings!" And they came to him, took hold of his feet, and worshiped him.

— MATTHEW 28:8-9

67. Because You Love Him

God can reject everything in a creature conceived in sin, who bears the indelible marks inherited from Adam, but He absolutely cannot reject the sincere desire to love Him. Therefore, if you cannot be sure of God's heavenly mercy and loving partiality toward you for other reasons ... you must at least be reassured by this.

Don't you still love Him? Don't you desire to love Him always? Have no fear then! Even if you were to have committed all the sins of this world, Jesus tells you, "Your sins, which are many, are forgiven, for you have loved much."

And a woman in the city, who was a sinner, having learned that [Jesus] was eating in the Pharisee's house, brought an alabaster jar of ointment. She stood behind him at his feet, weeping, and began to bathe his feet with her tears and to dry them with her hair. Then she continued kissing his feet and anointing them with the ointment. Now when the Pharisee who had invited him saw it, he said to himself, "If this man were a prophet, he would have known who and what kind of woman this is who is touching him — that she is a sinner." Jesus spoke up and said to him ... "A certain creditor had two debtors; one owed five hundred denarii, and the other fifty. When they could not pay, he canceled the debts for both of them. Now which of them will love him more?" Simon

answered, "I suppose the one for whom he canceled the greater debt."
And Jesus said to him, "You have judged rightly." Then turning toward
the woman, he said to Simon, "Do you see this woman? ... I tell you,
her sins, which were many, have been forgiven; hence she has shown
great love. But the one to whom little is forgiven, loves little."

— LUKE 7:37-40, 41-44, 47

68. ALL THINGS FOR YOUR GOOD

IT IS USELESS TO struggle against the will of the One who can
do all things.

Everything that takes place within you is the work of Jesus,
and you must believe this. You must not criticize the work of
the Lord, but rather, you must humbly submit yourself to this
divine work. Give total freedom to the workings of grace in
you, and remember never to be upset for any adverse event that
could happen to you, knowing that this would be an impedi-
ment to the divine Spirit.

Keep your affections subordinate to those of this so sublime
a Father; and beware of nurturing any affections, whatever they
might be, that are not marked with the seal of the heavenly
King. If possible, don't love the will of God merely when it conforms to yours, but rather love your will when — and because
— it conforms to that of God.

Bless God just the same, who does everything for the good of His chosen ones. Let us be consoled at this.

We know that all things work together for good for those who love God, who are called according to his purpose. — ROMANS 8:28

69. PONDER HIM

THE FATHER WISHES TO render you similar to the little Child of Bethlehem whose zeal for souls is incomparable. This heavenly Child comes to die in order to save, and it is his zeal, so humble, sweet, and lovable, that captures the hearts of those who pause a while to ponder Him.

Why did He assume this sweet and lovable state of the Child if not to make us love Him with confidence, and to lovingly confide in Him? Stay very close to the crib of this gentle Child…. Have a great love for this heavenly Infant. Be respectful in the familiarity you will gain with Him through prayer, and be joyful when you feel within you holy inspirations and the desire to be especially His.

When the angels had left them and gone into heaven, the shepherds said to one another, "Let us go now to Bethlehem and see this thing that has taken place, which the Lord has made known to us." So they went with haste and found Mary and Joseph, and the child lying in the manger.

When they saw this, they made known what had been told them about this child; and all who heard it were amazed at what the shepherds told them. But Mary treasured all these words and pondered them in her heart. — LUKE 2:15-19

70. SACRIFICES PLEASING TO GOD

OH, GOD HAS NOT excluded you from the enjoyment of His sweetness. He has only subtracted it for a while, so that you might live in Him and for Him, and not for this sweetness; in order that afflicted souls might find compassion and sweet and loving tolerance in you; and in order that, with a heart totally dead, resigned, and sacrificed, His divine Majesty might receive the pleasing odor of a little sacrificial offering.

Let us then go to him outside the camp and bear the abuse he endured. For here we have no lasting city, but we are looking for the city that is to come. Through him, then, let us continually offer a sacrifice of praise to God, that is, the fruit of lips that confess his name. Do not neglect to do good and to share what you have, for such sacrifices are pleasing to God.
— HEBREWS 13:13-16

71. WHEN CHRIST APPEARS

REMEMBER, FOOLISH ONE, that the lives of those who live according to the spirit of Jesus will not always remain hidden and unknown. Remember what it will be like in the future, in the Lord's Day: "When Christ who is our life appears, then you also will appear with him in glory" [Colossians 3:4].

Beloved, we are God's children now; what we will be has not yet been revealed. What we do know is this: when he is revealed, we will be like him, for we will see him as he is. And all who have this hope in him purify themselves, just as he is pure. — I JOHN 3:2-3

72. SLAVES OF GOD

HOW FORTUNATE WE ARE to be slaves of this great God who submitted Himself to death for us.

Let the same mind be in you that was in Christ Jesus,
who, though he was in the form of God,
did not regard equality with God
as something to be exploited,

but emptied himself,
  taking the form of a slave,
  being born in human likeness.
And being found in human form,
  he humbled himself
  and became obedient to the
    point of death —
  even death on a cross.

— Philippians 2:5–8

73. King and Lord of Your Heart

May the grace and peace of the Holy Spirit always be at the center of your heart. Place your heart in the open side of the Savior, and unite it with the King of your heart who is within it as on a royal throne, in order that He might receive homage and obedience from all other hearts. Keep your heart's door open, so that everyone can approach Him and gain an audience at all times.

May the King of all saints also be the King of your heart!

Do not fear what they fear, and do not be intimidated, but in your hearts sanctify Christ as Lord.
— 1 Peter 3:14–15

74. Heavenly Teacher

How fortunate we are to be held so tightly to our heavenly Teacher! We need do no more than we are doing at present; that is to love divine Providence and to abandon ourselves in His arms and Heart. Say to the Lord, "No, my God, I desire no greater pleasure than my faith, my hope, my love; to be able only to say sincerely, even if sometimes without feeling, that I would rather die than abandon this virtue. Ah, Lord, if it is Your will that I feel no pleasure in exercising the virtues that You conferred on me so benevolently, I willingly accept this, even though with a feeling of total repugnance."

Everyone who does not abide in the teaching of Christ, but goes beyond it, does not have God; whoever abides in the teaching has both the Father and the Son.
— 2 John 9

75. FOLLOWING JESUS

TAKE HEART, BECAUSE YOU gain merit climbing Calvary even without realizing it.

Then Jesus told his disciples, "If any want to become my followers, let them deny themselves and take up their cross and follow me. For those who want to save their life will lose it, and those who lose their life for my sake will find it. For what will it profit them if they gain the whole world but forfeit their life? Or what will they give in return for their life?

"For the Son of Man is to come with his angels in the glory of his Father, and then he will repay everyone for what has been done."

— MATTHEW 16:24-27

76. HIS WATCHFULNESS

ALL THE DISHEARTENING THOUGHTS that are running around in your mind, such as the idea that God may be punishing you for devotional practices carelessly performed, believe me, are nothing but temptations, which you must drive far from you, for it is by no means true that in all these things you have offended

God, since Jesus, by His watchful grace, has guarded you very well against all such offenses.

Be tranquil, and don't allow discouraging thoughts to pass the frontier of your heart.

> *Those who trust in him will understand truth,*
> *and the faithful will abide with him in love,*
> *because grace and mercy are upon his holy ones,*
> *and he watches over his elect.*

— WISDOM OF SOLOMON 3:9

77. IN THE END

INJUSTICE CANNOT TRIUMPH, and the injustice of men will serve for the triumph of the justice of God…. But we must be insistent with Jesus and His most holy Mother…. Let us knock with repeated blows so that, in the end, the door of Mercy will have to be opened wide.

> *Many seek the favor of a ruler,*
> *but it is from the LORD that one gets justice.*
> *The unjust are an abomination to the righteous,*
> *but the upright are an abomination to the wicked.*

— PROVERBS 29:26-27

78. DAILY WORK

WE MUST REDOUBLE OUR courage and raise our spirits to God, serving Him with greater diligence in everything that our vocation and Christian profession require of us. This alone, and nothing else, can render us pleasing to God and can enable us to escape being overturned and overcome by the big world, which is not of God, and by all other enemies. This alone, therefore, can make us arrive at the port of eternal salvation.

Let us do our duty in accordance with our state in life.... We must be Christian in our daily life and not just in name. Let us pray fervently, humbly, and perseveringly.

Holiness means living humbly, being disinterested, prudent, just, patient, kind, chaste, meek, diligent, carrying out our duties for no other reason than that of pleasing God and receiving from Him alone the reward we deserve.

Do your best to present yourself to God as one approved by him, a worker who has no need to be ashamed, rightly explaining the word of truth. — 2 TIMOTHY 2:15

79. BEAUTIFUL FACE OF SWEET JESUS

OH, HOW BEAUTIFUL IS the face of our most sweet Spouse, Jesus! Oh, how sweet His eyes. Oh, what happiness it is to stay close to Him on the Mount of His glory! We must place our desires and affections there, and not in creatures, in whom, even if beauty is present, it descends from on high.

May the sweet Jesus always rest in your heart, and may He let you rest at His feet.

... and in the midst of the lampstands I saw one like the Son of Man, clothed with a long robe and with a golden sash across his chest. His head and his hair were white as white wool, white as snow; his eyes were like a flame of fire, his feet were like burnished bronze, refined as in a furnace, and his voice was like the sound of many waters. In his right hand he held seven stars, and from his mouth came a sharp, two-edged sword, and his face was like the sun shining with full force. When I saw him, I fell at his feet as though dead. But he placed his right hand on me, saying, "Do not be afraid; I am the first and the last, and the living one. I was dead, and see, I am alive forever and ever; and I have the keys of Death and of Hades." — REVELATION 1:13-18

80. YOUR TEARS

LIVE CALMLY BECAUSE YOU will receive immense consolation. It will not be long before the Lord comes to dry your tears.

May those who sow in tears
reap with shouts of joy.
Those who go out weeping,
bearing the seed for sowing,
shall come home with shouts of joy,
carrying their sheaves.

— PSALM 126:5–6

81. FAMILY UNITED

HAVE BUT ONE HEART and one single expectation before Jesus, that is, to perfect yourselves in the ways of God. How healthy it is to be so united to each other! How good and joyful it is for all brothers and sisters to live in the same manner, with one aspiration. Thus sang the true prophet, and this is how it truly is. The union of souls is like the precious ointment which was spread on the supreme priest Aaron, as the true psalmist says once again elsewhere, in which there was so much perfumed oil that all breathed one single odor and sweetness. But I don't wish to dwell on this matter. What God has united by blood and sentiment is inseparable, as long as God reigns with you and your family, and He will reign there in eternity. Take heart, therefore; be sweet and lovable to all, humble and courageous, pure and sincere in everything.

Be like little spiritual bees, bringing nothing into their hives but honey and wax. May your home be full of sweetness, peace, agreement, humility, and piety as regards conversation.

For this reason I bow my knees before the Father, from whom every family in heaven and on earth takes its name. I pray that, according to the riches of his glory, he may grant that you may be strengthened in your inner being with power through his Spirit, and that Christ may dwell in your hearts through faith, as you are being rooted and grounded in love. I pray that you may have the power to comprehend, with all the saints, what is the breadth and length and height and depth, and to know the love of Christ that surpasses knowledge, so that you may be filled with all the fullness of God. — EPHESIANS 3:14-19

82. STEADFAST LOVE OF GOD

ESPECIALLY DO I ASK divine love for you. This is everything for us: it is the honey which must sweeten all our weaknesses, all our feelings, sufferings, and actions.

The righteous will see, and fear,
*   and will laugh at the evildoer, saying,*
"See the one who would not take
*   refuge in God,*
but trusted in abundant riches,
*   and sought refuge in wealth!"*

But I am like a green olive tree
*   in the house of God.*
I trust in the steadfast love of God
*   forever and ever.*

— PSALM 52:6–8

83. *RABBOUNI*, TEACHER DIVINE!

ONE DAY MARY MAGDALENE spoke to the divine Master, and believing she was separated from Him, she cried, asked Him about this, and was so anxious that even though seeing Him, she did not see Him, and she thought He was the gardener. This is what is happening in you also. Come on, have courage; do not be anxious about anything. You have the divine Master in your company; you have not been separated from Him. What are you afraid of? What are you complaining about? Take heart, therefore; you must be a child no longer.

But Mary [Magdalene] stood weeping outside the tomb. As she wept, she bent over to look into the tomb; and she saw two angels in white, sitting where the body of Jesus had been lying, one at the head and the other at the feet. They said to her, "Woman, why are you weeping?" She said to them, "They have taken away my Lord, and I do not know where they have laid him." When she had said this, she turned around and saw Jesus standing there, but she did not know that it was Jesus. Jesus said to her, "Woman, why are you weeping? Whom are you look-ing for?" Supposing him to be the gardener, she said to him, "Sir, if you have carried him away, tell me where you have laid him, and I will take him away." Jesus said to her, "Mary!" She turned and said to him in Hebrew, "Rabbouni!" (which means Teacher).... Mary Magdalene went and announced to the disciples, "I have seen the Lord."

—JOHN 20:11–16, 18

84. FOUNDATION AND ROOF

HUMILITY AND CHARITY ARE the main supports of the whole vast building on which all the rest depends. Keep firmly to these two virtues, one of which is the lowest and the other the highest. The preservation of the whole building depends on the foundation and the roof. If the heart is always striving to practice these two virtues, it will meet no difficulty in practicing the others. These are the two mothers of virtue, and the other virtues follow them, just as little chicks follow the mother hen.

I therefore, the prisoner in the Lord, beg you to lead a life worthy of the calling to which you have been called, with all humility and gentleness, with patience, bearing with one another in love, making every effort to maintain the unity of the Spirit in the bond of peace.

— EPHESIANS 4:1-3

85. ONE DAY IS LIKE A THOUSAND YEARS

ALWAYS TAKE CARE OF your soul and don't pay much attention to these years that pass, except to gain holy eternity. Live humbly, docile, and in love with our unique heavenly Spouse.

But do not ignore this one fact, beloved, that with the Lord one day is like a thousand years, and a thousand years are like one day. The Lord is not slow about his promise, as some think of slowness, but is patient with you, not wanting any to perish, but all to come to repentance. But the day of the Lord will come like a thief, and then the heavens will pass away with a loud noise, and the elements will be dissolved with fire, and the earth and everything that is done on it will be disclosed.

Since all these things are to be dissolved in this way, what sort of persons ought you to be in leading lives of holiness and godliness, waiting for and hastening the coming of the day of God, because of which the heavens will be set ablaze and dissolved, and the elements will melt with fire? But, in accordance with his promise, we wait for new heavens and a new earth, where righteousness is at home. — 2 PETER 3:8-13

86. ANSWERS

I THANK HIM FROM THE depths of my heart because I see clearly that it is precisely He who wants to test our fidelity and constancy. But we must trust in Him, because in the end, what we rightly ask will be granted.

"Truly I tell you, if you say to this mountain, 'Be taken up and thrown into the sea,' and if you do not doubt in your heart, but believe that what you say will come to pass, it will be done for you. So I tell you, whatever

you ask for in prayer, believe that you have received it, and it will be yours."
— MARK 11:23-24

87. DEVIL'S UPROAR

TEMPTATIONS SUCH AS THOSE of jealousy, desperation, discouragement, lack of faith, impurity, and infidelity are the merchandise offered by the enemy. But you repel them; therefore there is no harm, but only palms and crowns which the mercy of God, to which you are extremely dear, is accumulating, giving you untold strength with which to repel the enemy and his seductions. If the devil is making an uproar, it is an excellent sign. What is terrifying, on the other hand, is his peace and concord with a person's soul. You are wrong to say you are living in hell when you see yourself surrounded by those trials and darkness. You would do better to say you are in the midst of a burning bush. The bush is blazing, the air is clouded, and the soul sees nothing and understands nothing. But God speaks and is present to the soul who listens, understands, loves, and trembles [see Exodus 3:2-6].

Submit yourselves therefore to God. Resist the devil, and he will flee from you. Draw near to God, and he will draw near to you.

— JAMES 4:7-8

88. DO NOT FEAR GOD

I BESEECH YOU, FOR THE love of God, do not fear God, because He does not want to do you any harm at all. Love Him a great deal because He wants to do you a great deal of good. Walk simply, with certainty in your resolutions, and reject the reflections of spirit concerning your suffering, treating them as cruel temptations.

God is love, and those who abide in love abide in God, and God abides in them. Love has been perfected among us in this: that we may have boldness on the day of judgment, because as he is, so are we in this world. There is no fear in love, but perfect love casts out fear; for fear has to do with punishment, and whoever fears has not reached perfection in love. We love because he first loved us.　　— 1 JOHN 4:16-19

89. SOURCE OF GRACE

IN THE MOST HOLY Sacrament of the Eucharist, in this sacrament of Love, we have true life, a blessed life, and true happiness. Because in it we receive not only those graces that perfect us but the very Author of those graces.

"I am the bread of life. Your ancestors ate the manna in the wilderness, and they died. This is the bread that comes down from heaven, so that one may eat of it and not die. I am the living bread that came down from heaven. Whoever eats of this bread will live forever; and the bread that I will give for the life of the world is my flesh."

The Jews then disputed among themselves, saying, "How can this man give us his flesh to eat?" So Jesus said to them, "Very truly, I tell you, unless you eat the flesh of the Son of Man and drink his blood, you have no life in you. Those who eat my flesh and drink my blood have eternal life, and I will raise them up on the last day; for my flesh is true food and my blood is true drink." — JOHN 6:48-55

90. WHY JESUS CAME TO EARTH

ALWAYS REMEMBER THE REASON why the Son of God came to earth; that it was in order to save us. Jesus says that He came into the world not to save the just, but rather, sinners; not to cure the healthy, but to heal the sick [see Luke 5:31-32].... We must truly be mothers toward all those people who have sinned, and for this reason, have great care for them, because Jesus tells us that there is more festivity in heaven for the sinner who repents than for the perseverance of ninety-nine just people [see Luke 15:7]. These words of the Redeemer are truly comforting to many souls who, unfortunately, sin and who then want to repent and return to Jesus.

And as he sat at dinner in Levi's house, many tax collectors and sinners were also sitting with Jesus and his disciples — for there were many who followed him. When the scribes of the Pharisees saw that he was eating with sinners and tax collectors, they said to his disciples, "Why does he eat with tax collectors and sinners?" When Jesus heard this, he said to them, "Those who are well have no need of a physician, but those who are sick; I have come to call not the righteous but sinners."

— MARK 2:15-17

91. FOOT OF THE CROSS

IT IS NECESSARY TO always have courage, and if some fatigue or weakness of spirit comes upon you, run to the foot of the cross, place yourself amidst the heavenly perfumes, and you will undoubtedly be comforted and invigorated.

Oh, what a great need I feel to stay a while with the Marys, who have compassion on the dying Lord!

Meanwhile, standing near the cross of Jesus were his mother, and his mother's sister, Mary the wife of Clopas, and Mary Magdalene.

— JOHN 19:25

92. No Shipwreck

YOU ARE AFRAID OF being lost and of having already lost God, and you ask me where He is to be found. He is within you, and you are in Him! You are like the passenger shut up in his cabin on the ship, who doesn't see the ship or notice that it is moving. He's merely upset by its vibrations; he fears he'll be shipwrecked and that the ship will plunge to the bottom of the ocean. However, although he doesn't see it, he is on the ship, and although it seems to him the ship is standing still, it is actually moving and traveling several knots per hour. He's afraid it will sink and that the vibrations due to its movement are signs of imminent disaster, whereas the ship is afloat and vibrates precisely because it is breasting the waves and forging ahead. To this passenger who complains that he's at a standstill and so looks for a ship to rescue him, we can answer, "If you go out of your cabin for a moment into the open air, you'll see that you're on the ship, that it's afloat and forging ahead at great speed, and that it's vibrating because of the force with which it breasts and cleaves the waves." Have no fear, then, of shipwreck, and don't even ask where the Lord is, because in Him and in His arms no misfortune of any kind can befall us.

"And I will ask the Father, and he will give you another Advocate, to be with you forever. This is the Spirit of truth, whom the world cannot receive, because it neither sees him nor knows him. You know him, because he abides with you, and he will be in you.

"I will not leave you orphaned; I am coming to you. In a little while the world will no longer see me, but you will see me; because I live, you also will live. On that day you will know that I am in my Father, and you in me, and I in you." — JOHN 14:16-20

93. FAITH CONQUERS CHAOS AND THE WORLD

LET THE INFERNAL LION tempt you. The apostle cries out to you, "Resist through faith in God" [1 Peter 5:9]. This, then, is the resistance to have against the roaring lion: faith. Live tranquilly, because you live in God's tabernacle and not in that of sinners. What do you fear? Your fear is like that of a child held tightly in the arms of its mother. The chaos you see is not real.

For the love of God is this, that we obey his commandments. And his commandments are not burdensome, for whatever is born of God conquers the world. And this is the victory that conquers the world, our faith. Who is it that conquers the world but the one who believes that Jesus is the Son of God? — I JOHN 5:3-5

94. BOUND TOGETHER
BY THE SAVIOR'S BLOOD

How STRONG WE WILL be if we continue to keep ourselves
bound, one to the other, through the bond colored with the
Savior's red blood, because nobody will be able to assail your
heart without finding resistance both from my heart and from
yours.

*The cup of blessing that we bless, is it not a sharing in the blood of
Christ? The bread that we break, is it not a sharing in the body of
Christ? Because there is one bread, we who are many are one body, for
we all partake of the one bread.* — 1 CORINTHIANS 10:16-17

95. CONSUMING US WITH THE FIRE
OF HIS GRACE

COME ON, WE MUST humble ourselves greatly, seeing that we
are not masters of ourselves, to any great extent, and that we
greatly love comfort and rest. Always keep Jesus present in your
mind. He did not come to rest or in order to have comfort,
either spiritual or temporal, but to fight, humble Himself, and

die. Hold this divine Model tightly to your heart, so that your soul, already pierced with heavenly love, can breathe the sacred words of the loving soul, "My beloved is mine and I am his. He will dwell in my breast" [Song of Solomon 1:13]. And let it be so, forever, that this divine Love may always dwell on our breast, inflaming and consuming us with His grace.

Therefore, since we are receiving a kingdom that cannot be shaken, let us give thanks, by which we offer to God an acceptable worship with reverence and awe; for indeed our God is a consuming fire.

— HEBREWS 12:28–29

96. EVIL WILL TIRE

DIABOLICAL SUGGESTIONS, INFIDELITY, AND incredulity; ah, these cannot come from God. His heart is too pure to conceive such horrible things. Do you know what God does in such cases? He permits the evil trickster to present us with such things in order to sell them to us so that we, through our despising them, can show our affection for divine matters. Why, therefore, should we become anxious and distressed for this? Dear God, no! It is the devil who wanders around our spirit, rummaging about and causing confusion, trying to find an open door if he can. The devil did the same to Job; to the great apostle of the people, Paul; to St. Anthony; to St. Catherine of Siena; and to many other good souls whom I know and whom I don't know. It even happened to my own soul, which is not worth much. But should we become saddened for all this? By all means, let Satan show himself to be what he is. Keep all the entrances to your heart well closed. Protest before God that you seek nothing except Him and what leads you to Him. Satan will tire, and if he doesn't, God will make him remove his siege.

Discipline yourselves, keep alert. Like a roaring lion your adversary the devil prowls around, looking for someone to devour. Resist him, steadfast in your faith, for you know that your brothers and sisters in all the world are undergoing the same kinds of suffering. And after you have suffered for a little while, the God of all grace, who has called you to his eternal glory in Christ, will himself restore, support, strengthen, and establish you. To him be the power forever and ever. Amen.

— 1 PETER 5:8-11

97. FLY TO HIM AND TASTE

WHEN YOU PRAY, IF your soul wants to fly, let it fly and do not prevent it from doing so. If it wants to move, let it move, even though its present tranquility and simple rest — in seeing God, in flying to Him and tasting Him — is excellent. Pay great attention to this virtue. Practice this truth and virtue a great deal in your heart.

> *O taste and see that the LORD is good;*
> *happy are those who take refuge in him.*

— PSALM 34:8

98. REJOICE ALWAYS

MAKE EVERY EFFORT TO adorn both your interior and exterior conversations with sincerity, sweetness, and joy, following the apostle's advice, "Rejoice in the Lord always; again I will say, Rejoice. Let all men know your gentleness" [Philippians 4:4-5].

Where, then, is your real unworthiness and sinfulness of heart? You may be horrified, certainly, by the sight of what you might have been — and still could be — but rejoice also in this state, and thank God and His divine Mercy that you are not what you might have been.

May He be forever blessed in all our miseries and in all our suffering. Bless Him in all that He makes you suffer on this earth and rejoice at it, for each victory gained has a corresponding crown in Paradise.

Let eternal Goodness take care of things, and rejoice!

Rejoice in the Lord always; again I will say, Rejoice. Let your gentleness be known to everyone. The Lord is near. Do not worry about anything, but in everything by prayer and supplication with thanksgiving let your requests be made known to God. And the peace of God, which surpasses all understanding, will guard your hearts and your minds in Christ Jesus.

— Philippians 4:4-7

99. Cold, Tired, Heavy Heart

Tell me, wasn't the sweet Jesus born in the heart of the cold? And why will He not remain there, in the coldness of your heart? I mean in the coldness which does not consist in our neglecting any of our good resolutions, but simply in a certain tiredness and heaviness of spirit, which causes us to walk in a painful manner on the path where we have placed ourselves, and from which we never want to depart, until we reach the port, heaven.

Even youths will faint and be weary,
*   and the young will fall exhausted;*
but those who wait for the LORD shall renew their strength,
*   they shall mount up with wings like eagles,*
they shall run and not be weary,
*   they shall walk and not faint.*

— Isaiah 40:30-31

100. WHEREVER YOU GO

RELY ON JESUS FOR everything and all will work out well.

After all, hasn't Jesus been faithful to you up to this moment? Well, then, don't have any doubts about the future. It may be more difficult for you, undoubtedly, but Jesus' help will never be lacking to you. Courage, therefore, and go ahead!

"I hereby command you: Be strong and courageous; do not be frightened or dismayed, for the LORD your God is with you wherever you go."

— JOSHUA 1:9

ACKNOWLEDGMENTS

Excerpts from Padre Pio's writings are used by permission (with minor modifications) from the following:

- *Padre Pio of Pietrelcina Letters, Volume One*, English version edited by Father Gerardo Di Flumeri, O.F.M. Cap. (Editions Padre Pio da Pietrelcina, Our Lady of Grace Capuchin Friary [Foggia], Italy), copyright © 1984.
- *Padre Pio of Pietrelcina Letters, Volume Two*, English version edited by Father Gerardo Di Flumeri, O.F.M. Cap. (Editions Padre Pio da Pietrelcina, Our Lady of Grace Capuchin Friary [Foggia], Italy), copyright © 1987.
- *Padre Pio of Pietrelcina Letters, Volume Three*, English version edited by Father Gerardo Di Flumeri, O.F.M. Cap. (Editions Padre Pio da Pietrelcina, Our Lady of Grace Capuchin Friary [Foggia], Italy), copyright 2001.

These books are available from the National Centre for Padre Pio, 111 Barto Road, Barto, PA 19504.

ABOUT THE COMPILER

Eileen Dunn Bertanzetti is an author and teacher, who knows that whatever good she does is done by God's grace — through Our Lady, St. Padre Pio, and her guardian angel. Eileen lives in Pennsylvania with her husband, Greg, who is also her clarinet and piano teacher; with her two pampered cats; and with her miniature poodle, who boldly barks away the black bears that dare to wander into the backyard.

Listening to God . . .

FROM
OUR SUNDAY VISITOR

❖ ❖ ❖

**Listening to God with Blessed John Paul II
(Inventory No. T1196)**

**Listening to God with Mother Teresa
(Inventory No. T1094)**

❖ ❖ ❖

OUR SUNDAY VISITOR
1-800-348-2440
WWW.OSV.COM